THE NEW ART OF LOVING

Born in Montreal, Canada, in 1953, Mark Fisher studied philosophy and literature, and went on to have his first book published when he was 25. He practises yoga and meditation, and travels extensively in the United States and Europe. His aim with his books is to help readers to find the keys of inspiration and motivation for their lives.

By the same author

The Instant Millionaire

THE NEW ART OF
LOVING

Mark Fisher

Revised by

Wayne Johnson and George Ferenci

ELEMENT BOOKS

© Mark Fisher 1989

First published in Great Britain 1989 by
Element Books Limited
Longmead, Shaftesbury, Dorset

Printed and bound in Great Britain by
Billings, Hylton Road, Worcester

Designed by Jenny Liddle
Cover design by Max Fairbrother
Cover illustration by Siggi Grunow/Image Bank

British Library Cataloguing in Publication Data
Fisher, Mark, 1953–
    The new art of loving.
    1. Love – Philosophical perspectives
    I. Title   II. Johnson, Wayne   III. Ferenci, George
    128′.3

ISBN 1–85230–105–8

To Gurumayi

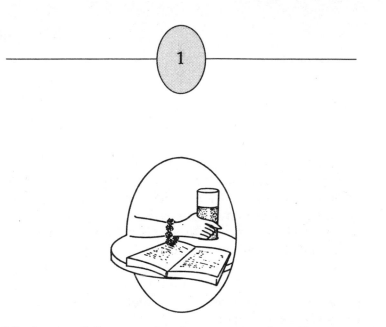

Maybe our fights are what kept us together. Because, after three years in a rather stormy relationship, just when we seemed to have worked out our problems, she left me.

She told me she had met someone else. But I don't think that was the 'real' reason. I don't think she even knew why she wanted to get away. Love is like a virus. When you're cured, it's gone. A good enough reason, I guess.

Anyway, I didn't feel much like arguing with her. I was too stunned, or perhaps I'd secretly wanted the break-up. Instead of immediately trying to get involved with another woman, I felt a need for a pause, an interlude, to take stock of myself and my love life.

Initially, I came to a somewhat pessimistic conclusion, but one which seemed inescapably clear to me: my love life was a failure. A real dud. How had I come to this conclusion?

Quite simply, when I had considered everything –
all my expectations, all my hopes, my dreams, and
what had come of them: bitterness, sadness, and
aggravation, not to mention tedium, that most fatal of
all love's ills – the picture was hardly reassuring.

Yet I'd known many admirable women. What
made that heady taste of new love ever so fleeting?
And why did the joys that lend love its magic – the
fantasy, the sensuality, 'her' ineffable presence –
vanish like the morning dew?

In my confusion, it was this I was struggling with.
And since I think best when I'm writing, I decided to
put my reflections, my thoughts, and recollections
down in a notebook, a diary.

I began with the following premise:

ALL DISORDER IS BUT AN APPEARANCE
WHICH CONCEALS AN UNDERLYING ORDER.

If that is true, it was only my blindness, my short-
sightedness, that prevented me from understanding
the reasons for my disappointments.

Perhaps trying to discover the laws of love was
overly ambitious. Isn't love, by definition, incomprehensible? Not to say, absurd? To fathom its nature
doomed? But I took solace in the thought that if I did
not succeed, at least I would be able to put my life
together again.

When we are in pain, often what makes us suffer

most, what outrages us, are those things we cannot explain. If we understand the reasons for our misfortune, see it in terms of cause and effect, it is easier to bear. And, in the end, isn't it only truth that can free us and bring us happiness?

I began writing my diary. But my muse abandoned me. I couldn't write. I grew more and more frustrated until I couldn't take it any more.

I went out to a local café. I thought I'd spend a few hours there. And take the time to decide whether or not I was ready to end my fruitless solitude, and try to start my life all over again.

As I entered the café, I noticed her immediately. We exchanged glances. And I thought, 'She smiled.' Something about her, perhaps the same mysterious quality that had attracted me to other women, drew me to her.

About thirty, with short, black hair and beautiful aquiline features, this woman had about her a most unusual aura. A force seemed to radiate from her, almost as if she were aglow. There was an intensity about her that betrayed great strength. But most remarkable of all were her deep blue eyes, strikingly brilliant.

She was dressed conservatively, but elegantly. Despite my immediate attraction, and the fact that she seemed to be alone, I was reluctant to go right over. She was absorbed in reading a small book.

I ordered a Perrier, and glanced absent-mindedly

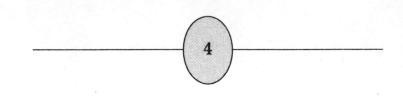

through the newspaper I'd brought with me. After hesitating for some time, I asked this mysterious woman, 'Is it interesting?'

'Yes', was all she replied, but her smile was friendly, and hinted at more.

She didn't immediately return to her book. Perhaps I wasn't disturbing her. Becoming bolder, I asked if I could join her. She agreed at once.

As I sat down, I suddenly felt an uneasiness. It was odd, and not like that nervousness which sometimes comes when you're with a woman you're fond of.

She sensed I was uncomfortable. To make me feel more at ease, she carried on with the conversation and asked if I often came to the café.

'Yes', I replied, 'but I haven't seen you here before.'

'It's my first time here.'

Even though she was smiling so benignly at me, there was something, an unsettling quality, about her. There was something uncanny. She said nothing and seemed quite content, without the habitual need to talk that overtakes us when with someone new.

'My Master asked me to come here this afternoon', she said. 'I was supposed to meet someone at two o'clock. By the way, what time is it?'

I checked my watch, and a shiver ran down my spine. It was exactly two. 'What a strange coincidence', I thought, and managed an awkward smile.

'It's two on the dot', I said.
She then surprised me by announcing, 'I have to leave now.'

'Already? But didn't you say you had to meet someone here?'

'Yes. But apparently he hasn't come. That, or he's come and gone. In any case, I can't stay any longer. My brothers are in town, and are waiting for me. But before I leave I'd like to share something with you.'

She opened her book and read,

EACH TIME WE SUFFER, IT'S BECAUSE WE HAVE VIOLATED THE SUPREME LAW OF LOVE.

She closed her book and got up to leave.

'I'd like to see you again', I said. 'Oh, I don't even know your name.'

'Maitri', she replied.

'Maitri? I'm Leonard', I said, and then asked her, 'What's your phone number?'

'I'm staying with some friends, so I'm not sure I should be giving it out.'

'Well, what are you doing tomorrow? Or ...?'

'When we're meant to see one another again, we will. Only those of little faith have to plan ahead.'

'I'd like to read your book.'

'Perhaps some other time. Don't worry. We'll see each other again.'

She shook my hand, and left. I hesitated, then I decided to follow, run after her. I paid the bill, hurried out of the door, and looked for her. She was nowhere in sight. It was as if she'd vanished.

I went back inside. The waiter hadn't cleared the table yet. My cup was still there. But hers had gone. Oh? Was I dreaming? Hallucinating? Had a few days cooped up alone unbalanced my mind? But I wasn't crazy! Was I?

I headed home, wrapped up in my thoughts. Who was this strange woman with such an unusual name? (By chance, two days later I was reading a book on Buddhism and surprisingly came upon the word 'maitri'. I discovered it means 'compassion'.)

Who was her Master?

Was this enchantress nothing but a scheming liar? A manipulative woman trying to mesmerise me, then trap me with mind control?

Whoever she was, she had left a profound impression on me. I had the funny feeling that I'd finally met someone really happy. And, therefore, infinitely more advanced than I.

In the final analysis, what distinguishes us most?

What is that true mark of superiority? Is it fame?
Fortune? Beauty? Power? Is it all those conventional
dreams, or is it just being happy?

When I got home, I immediately started to write
down everything that happened. But first, I read over
what I'd written the day before.

> All my life, I always thought I was free. Freedom
> seemed essential to my happiness. Perhaps that's
> why I've always been so sceptical about marriage.
> And because I don't need much in the way of material
> things, the usual dream of living the good life has
> never tempted me to give up what I value most – *my
> time.*
>
> Sometimes I even wonder if I'm not a woman in a
> man's body. Because I care so much about love, and
> not about my situation, my house, my car ... In fact I
> could live alone on an island as long as I had books,
> something to write with, and that most rare of all
> species, a truly loving woman.
>
> I've always tried to live by a code, my own set of
> principles and values. But ... if I'm honest with
> myself, there's a powerful force in me that governs
> everything I do and think. So I ask myself: 'How free
> am I?'

In his book, *In Search of the Miraculous*, Ouspensky
writes:

> Everything that people do is connected with sex:
> politics, religion, art, the theatre, music, all is 'Sex'. Do

you think that people go to the theatre or to churches
to pray, or to see some new play? That is only for the
sake of appearance. The principal thing in the thea-
ters, as well as the churches, is that there will be a lot
of women and a lot of men. That is the center of
gravity of all gatherings. What do you think brings
people to cafés, restaurants, to all various fêtes? One
thing only, Sex: it is the principal motive for all
mechanicalness. All sleep, all hypnosis, depends from
this.

These pages inspired me to write the following
thoughts:

But what is behind this obsession with sexuality that
prevents me from being free? There is something still
deeper, and in a way more tragic. It is despair, a
fundamental anguish, a secret yearning to break the
circle of my solitude.
   But each new relationship proves a disappointment.
True union with the Other never takes place, and I'm
left bitter, angry. Could it be I seek in the Other
something that cannot be found there? What would
happen if I stopped desperately searching for *her*? At
least for a while?
I'm so easily distracted, and led astray. And if I lose
her? If she goes away? If *she* disappears? What am 'I'
running away from? Why am I so scared? Am I afraid
of being alone? Why?
   Am I so empty? So boring that I can't bear to be
alone even for a few days? Who do I see in the mirror?
What is it? Tell me!
   When I'm with *her*, I talk and talk. And I forget
myself. I stop thinking about my solitude. Who am I

kidding? It's just one of those things I don't want to face.

But aren't we really always alone? Even during the most intimate moments, even during lovemaking? Men and women want to travel through life together. With all our technological know-how, hasn't anyone yet invented *the* magic elixir that can make it all happen?

Why not?

A few days ago, everything seemed so clear. Now, there's a fog. My words sound hollow. Nothing makes any sense.

Except that I'm obsessed and keep hearing what Maitri said before she left, 'Each time we suffer, it's because we've violated the Supreme Law of Love'.

Out of the blue, I remembered an old love affair that had caused me much suffering. Her name was Sarah. We'd been childhood friends. So by the time we went out together, I'd known her for years. Right from the start, I felt I had some hold over her, which surprised me.

I decided to take advantage of it, even though I shouldn't have. I sort of liked her, at least, physically. In that respect, she was quite attractive and had the most divine body. But I found her rather dull.

For no real reason, I harboured a secret contempt for her. I ask you, how is it we can hate a woman who loves us, who is kind to us, who is not the least bit demanding, who has never caused us any real problem?

I can't figure it out. And unfortunately, I started hating her even during lovemaking, when her face looked grotesque to me. I wasn't making love to her, but chastising her for some sin she hadn't committed. Yet, in her ecstasy, she would cry out her love for me.

Did I actually despise her? Or myself, for not being able to accept her sincere and poignant love? But I must stop and consider. Isn't there always an element of hate mixed up in desire? No matter how subtle or disguised it may be?

When the Buddha, the Enlightened One, was asked about the nature of Nirvana, the state of Supreme Bliss and Liberation, he replied: 'It is the extinction of desire, the extinction of hatred, the extinction of illusion.'

Desire and hatred? How closely are the two intertwined? Is there something to be drawn from this? If there were no desire, would there be hate? And, conversely, if there were no hate, could we feel desire for another?

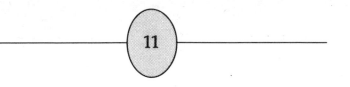

If I were perfectly happy and found complete contentment within myself, I would feel no need whatsoever for the Other. I would have no desire for the Other. So it is precisely because I am unhappy that I turn to the Other.

And, no matter how optimistic I may appear to be, what I bring to her, inescapably, is my unhappiness, the deep resentment I feel, given my inability to find fulfilment except through her. Even as I caress her, her most perfect breasts, hatred lies concealed in my hands. And the kisses I place on her ruby lips carry betrayal – not only betrayal of myself, but of the woman I claim to love.

If I follow Buddha, will I ever really be able to love another? Will that be possible before all hate is extinguished in me, and with it all desire? Is true love possible in a life which is not absolutely pure? And since, like those around me, I am unable to give up sensual pleasure, am I condemned to despise any woman who shares my life?

Hegel said, 'Each consciousness seeks the death of the Other.' Are lovers any exception? Even when I loved most sincerely, wasn't my goal the death of the Other? Didn't I want to bend her will to mine, even though I am, or at least consider myself to be, deeply liberal in thought?

When a man carries a woman into ecstasy, can he resist the belief that he has power over her? And when a woman kindles unbridled passion in a man, doesn't she feel that she controls and dominates him, and that, in a way, she has been granted her secret wish – his death?

Is it any wonder, then, that love always ends unhappily? Aren't all relationships doomed from the start, harbouring within them the insidious venom that sooner or later will take its lethal toll? Because our hearts, as vile and corrupt as Pascal claimed, cannot be purged by sensual delights?

And when we lure a woman with our passion, when we claim her love, isn't it our hatred that drives us to do so? By seeking 'to possess' her physically, aren't we seeking to 'dispossess' her? Take away her freedom? And rob her of the opportunity, so precious and yet so neglected, to find in herself, and in herself alone, the solitude that announces enlightenment, and true happiness?

With Sarah, I would know such unbearable misery. The first few weeks, we saw each other constantly. Then she informed me that she wasn't happy with me. She had realised, she said, that I didn't love her, wasn't the man for her, and she felt it'd be 'for the best' if we split up. 'From now on, just friends. No more sex!'

Surprisingly, instead of leaving me indifferent or, at best, bruising my pride, her announcement came as a terrible blow. In fact, I was devastated.

I protested, 'You can't do this to me! I love you!'

'OK!', I argued, 'I didn't say it before, but that was

only because I was unemotional and y'know, unable to express my true feelings, darling.'

She refused to be swayed, and stood by her decision. For several weeks, I sent her the most passionate love letters, imploring her to accept, at least, a temporary reconciliation.

As if some inherent justice were at work, ultimately balancing the love we give and the love we receive, I was now ready to match the loving that Sarah had shown me during our brief time together. Her indifference, I suppose, was her way of paying me back.

Fortunately, we manage to survive and get over our afflictions, painful though they are at the time. We have a tendency simply to forget.

Time, the best cure-all, does wonders. 'We just have to let *it* pass', family and friends remind us. And they're right. After a couple more weeks, if I thought of Sarah at all it was as a dark shadow following me about, once upon a time long ago.

Oddly enough, in retrospect, I feel a kind of tenderness for Sarah. Yes, she had made me suffer, but she had also given me a golden opportunity to learn more about myself, much more than I could have learned by reading some essay on love.

Isn't it true that from the lessons we learn from our past – from what we have suffered and tried to forget, but still remains engraved on our hearts – comes that true wisdom which allows us to side-step the petty problems of everyday life?

I'd relive those moments I'd spent with Sarah, and wonder, 'Why? Why, if I couldn't stand looking at her, if I felt so ambivalent towards her, why did she leave me tied up in knots? In such terrible pain?'

I was eventually struck by this question: for a man–woman relationship to succeed, shouldn't man's desire for the woman be secondary, a result, an outgrowth, of his love for her?

And shouldn't man first fall in love with the inner woman? Shouldn't he be enraptured by the core of her being, her essence, and let the magic of desire come later? A tie to bind their closeness?

I am toying with an idea, a formula for love. Perhaps it is unrealistic. And even with all these ideas buzzing around in my head, something has just come to me. As far back as I can remember, right back to when I first fell in love, hadn't I always seen a woman, looked at her face, and then started loving her? I was attracted and seduced by her eyes, her lips,

her ... God knows! Had I ever fallen in love with a woman when I wasn't physically attracted to her?

But what is it about the face? Is it a call? A recall?

The call of some ideal beauty? The sign of the sublime which we unconsciously dream of? Or the recall of some face seen long ago? Of another woman we loved as a child, in the distant past? In a previous life?

If we are attracted to one face rather than to another, the face offers us a clue. One that allows us to recognise a soul from another lifetime.

Or are we drawn into its orbit in order to accomplish certain things destiny has in store for us? Or is it to settle some account of long ago?

And isn't it for the same reason, but in the opposite sense, that a woman soon loses her beauty in our eyes when we begin to drift away from her, even though the reality of her beauty remains unchanged? She is now outside the circle (which is often magical only for us) that made her so inexplicably attractive. We have fulfilled with her what we were intended to fulfil. And in her eyes, we've probably lost our beauty as well. All this in what must be one of love's saddest permutations.

I was desperately seeking someone else. And then I met Susan, at a little Italian restaurant. She was a gorgeous blonde with magical (or were they devilish) eyes. She was a talented painter who couldn't get a major gallery to show her work.

As soon as I saw her, I had the strong feeling this was the woman I had been waiting for! And I'd marry her, no matter what! I'm not sure why I immediately fell for her. I guess I just never imagined any woman could be so divine. And that explains why I was still single.

Getting a date with her wasn't easy. After an hour of small talk, I just blurted out, 'There's something I've got to tell you. It's a bit absurd, really crazy. But ... I've never said this to anyone else. I'm sure it's not the best move. But I can't help it. When I saw you at the restaurant, do you know how I felt? I felt like marrying you right then'n there. On the spot.'

I surprised her. She smiled, and asked, 'Is that a proposal? You're asking me to marry you?'

I *was* the one who asked her. But, well, I wasn't ready to go ahead with it. Still, I said, 'Yes, I am.'

'And if I say "Yes", what'll you do then?'

'Well, make the arrangements. Set the date. Next Saturday, if you like.'

She seemed even more amused. 'We barely know each other', she said. 'But my intuition says, "Wait!" Maybe I'm not the first ...'

'I didn't plan this. It's just ... you're *so* beautiful. The most beautiful woman in America!'

'In the world', she corrected me.

'And so modest. And ... as soon as I saw you, I thought, "That's *her*! My soul-mate! The one I've been waiting for!" I know it sounds crazy. I feel so ...

stupid. Don't get me wrong. You could look different. Less pretty. Like someone else. But I'm glad you look the way you do. Am I making any sense?'

Before she could say anything, I reached over and kissed her twice, once on each temple.

She didn't say, 'No'. She just smiled, as if amused. But I was so excited. I don't know what came over me.

'You must think I'm crazy. I should shut up.'

'No, it's fine. Love terrifies most people. It's good to express your feelings.'

We kept talking until I remembered I had reserved a table for two. 'I insist', I said, but she said she had to go to see a girlfriend who was a bit depressed.

'Call me', she said, and gave me her phone number. I walked her to her car. I kissed her on both cheeks, then on the lips.

'When's the wedding?' she said, teasing me.

'Oh, we better wait a few weeks 'n see? OK?'

And then she drove off.

Things didn't go as I'd hoped. She gave me a pretty hard time. She was rarely free to go out. We spent most of the time we were in touch in talking on the telephone.

She was being cautious, to say the least. She seemed in no hurry to get involved, and was perhaps all the more afraid since I'd proposed marriage right away.

I was sincere. But it was just a joke to her. Then

again, my declaration came so fast, how could any woman take me seriously?

I wondered, 'What should I do? Give up? Go back to brooding about love?'

Requited love is so rare. How many times have I been loved by women I didn't love? As often as I have loved women who haven't loved me!

With Susan, I did it all wrong. I made it clear I didn't want to play games. So, she didn't want to play, and that was that. *Que sera, sera.* But, in a way, I felt I did what I had to.

I thought about it, and it still didn't look good. Anyone else would have called it quits. The more I thought about her, the more I thought that she was no ordinary woman. Perhaps she'd been hurt. So much so, that maybe she no longer believed in love?

Anyway, I should have known right from the start. If I was getting nowhere fast, perhaps it was simply because *she* wasn't interested. It was so obvious, I'd overlooked it. Never mind our romantic notions being anything but rational. Rejection is the hardest thing to accept.

And perhaps destiny only wanted me to *think* she was the woman of my dreams. To propose to her and humiliate myself, and never even have sex with her?

But love is like a fever. We have no way of knowing in advance if we'll catch it. Or when it will stop! Still, I was so blind I couldn't see that it's only natural for those we pursue to flee from us. Surely the only way to end the flight is to end the pursuit.

I soon had to face the truth. The next time I saw Susan, I brought her a gift, a little bracelet of heart-shaped green aventurines. She was pleased, but more than anything else embarrassed, because she had agreed to meet me with the resolution of putting to an end my hopes and dreams.

I asked what she thought about *us*, what she saw ahead in the stars, the future. In other words, could I look forward to a serious, more meaningful relationship with her? She replied that she preferred to remain friends.

And, probably to ease my pain, she added that it was not because of me – which is what we always say to avoid hurting people when we are not interested. Anyway, she couldn't handle another relationship right now. She was still getting over a recent separation.

Then she asked me if I wanted the bracelet back. But I insisted, 'Keep it'.

On my way home, I thought, what a horrible mistake! One of mistaken identity. I remembered what the Greek philosopher Plato wrote, 'Love is a sickness of the mind.'

Yes, I was sick, love-sick. But did I really want to be cured? Is it possible without getting bored, to death?

To forget, I threw myself once more into the task of writing all of this down in my diary. But ... What a

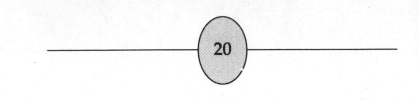
sham! What a sorry excuse for a writer I am!

How could I dare to shed light on a subject so delicate, and yet so complex, as love? It was insane! It was nuts! Especially since I'd just made a complete fool of myself! Ah!

As absurd as it was and dark as my thoughts were, I wrote the following down:

> Ma Amanda Moyi wrote, 'In this world, there is nothing, yet everyone seems to be pursuing this nothing.'

Why had I met Susan? What was the real meaning or purpose behind our meeting? Was there any? Or was it the pursuit of nothing? The nothingness my imagination had inflated and given far too much importance to? A nothingness that had resulted only in heartache for me, and that was tiresome and bothersome to her?

Or was it the first time I had fallen head over heels

in love? And, troubled as I was, I kept asking myself, 'Am I destined to spend the rest of my life without the only woman I have really and truly loved?'

As I have in the past, I turned for advice to the ancient Roman emperor, Marcus Aurelius, who also happened to be a philosopher. I find his *Meditations* are like beacons of light in the darkness of my existence; his words soothe my wounds.

I opened the book at random, or should I say, I let the book open itself? Whatever the case, I found myself on the pages I'd read and contemplated most often. Once again, I copied certain passages into my journal, which was becoming a kind of ritual.

Like the monks who devote their lives to writing the name of God over and over again, for hours on end, or a magician repeating some incantation for its effect, I hope that the wisdom of Aurelius, sublime and eternal, may help me see more clearly:

> Everything is as you perceive it to be, and this perception is within your control. Renounce it if you wish, and you will reach calm waters, like the ship that rounds the headland to find a tranquil sea, a peaceful haven.

Is the importance I give to this woman who refused me, despite my sincerity, anything other than a 'perception'? Isn't what happened only in my mind, and in my mind alone? Even having given this woman power over my life? Even if I know this to be true, how do I free myself from this 'perception'? Aurelius writes:

> If you are distressed by something external, it is not that thing which troubles you, but your own estimation of it. And you have the power to revoke this judgement at any time.
> But when you are distressed by something which is in your own character, what prevents you from changing it yourself?

Perhaps I'd made a key error, one I could have avoided, if I had understood the meaning of the wise emperor's words:

> You shame yourself, my soul, you shame yourself, and you will have no more chance to respect yourself. Each life is so brief. Yours is nearing its close, and still you do not respect yourself, allowing your happiness to depend on the souls of others.

Shouldn't every book on love begin and end with this sublime message? Isn't it this lack of self-respect that misguided me in all my loves, and that will lead me to wander aimlessly until death?

Feeling helpless, I turned to this passage for a boost:

> Be like the headland against which the waves break. It remains unmoved, while around it the turbulent waters become stilled.
> Do not say, 'How unhappy I am because such a thing

happened to me!' Say instead, 'How lucky I am to endure such a thing without bitterness, unshaken by the present and not frightened by what lies ahead.'

When a love affair crumbles or a woman leaves (even if we wanted her to go), in the torment of this amorous indignation we feel, could we find more sound advice?

> Remember. Everything that happens to you happens for a good reason. Look and see it is so. Not just the pattern, but according to what is only right, as if someone were giving each person what they deserved.

And when the agonies of love seem too much to bear, what better refuge than these words:

> Soon you will have forgotten everything. Soon everything will have forgotten you.

Yes, there is a certain comfort in reading this. I can accept that everything that happens to me is justified, but why I couldn't have something more with Susan still escapes me. I did everything I could! I showed her how I felt! So, why didn't it work out? Why didn't she love me?

'Oh,' I prayed, 'for a few hours to forget my pain!' Before I stopped writing and fell asleep, I came across these lines from Aurelius:

How vividly you come to realise that no condition is as favourable to the practice of philosophy as the one in which you now find yourself.

Perhaps there was still hope. And out of the ashes of this terrible love, a new flame might appear?

The next morning, I returned to my diary, but was unable to write. My muse was gone. I tried to be rational. I tried to read what I'd written about Susan, about us. But I couldn't!

So, I chucked it. Abandoning it, I went to the café where I'd met Maitri, with the vague hope of seeing her again. She was there, alone, at the same table! I went over. She recognised me, and greeted me with a warm smile.

I can't tell you how happy I was! I just felt so good. I didn't love her – not the 'I'm crazy about you!' kind I'd known up to then. Nor the sexual, purely physical lusting for the body. But she was so beautiful and charming.

She invited me to join her. 'Can I order you something to drink?' she asked, in that unaffected way of hers.

'Some white wine', I said.

'To chase away your dark thoughts?' she said playfully.

I smiled, 'Yes.'

'So?' she asked. 'Is love treating you any better?'

'No,' I admitted, 'it went wrong.'

'Tell me about it', she said.

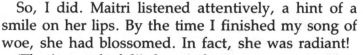

So, I did. Maitri listened attentively, a hint of a smile on her lips. By the time I finished my song of woe, she had blossomed. In fact, she was radiant!

'That's wonderful!' she cried, to my great surprise. 'You're so lucky! You found *her*! The one you've been waiting for!'

'What?' I wondered. Why wasn't she feeling sorry for me? Or trying to reassure me?

'Do you love this woman?' Maitri asked me.

Did she want to shock me? Her eyes were intently fixed on mine, waiting for me to say something. Her face was like a blank page for me to write on. Suddenly, I felt as though my sincerity, my love for Susan, was in question. Maitri had turned everything upside-down.

'Why ...?' I stammered. 'I just told you. I even asked her to marry me.'

'But do you love her?' Maitri insisted on an answer.

'That's what I want to know!'

Again, it was as if she pierced me with a sword that cut me to the core.

'Yes', I exclaimed, despite the fact that I was no longer sure, '*I love her*! In fact, *I'm crazy about her*!'

'Very good. So, if you love her, what are you complaining about? Shouldn't you be happy? It's a gift from heaven.'

Again, I was confused. I hadn't expected any of this. She was trying to trick me. She had a knack for confusing me. But ... was she toying with me? Or was her conception of love so different from mine that I didn't understand a thing?

'The woman,' I stressed, 'I've been waiting for all my life has just rejected me!'

'If she really is the woman for you, she will surely come to you. And if she isn't, why be sad about it? Being afraid is always a mistake.'

Her relentless logic had me stymied.

'Who knows?' she went on. 'Maybe you love this woman because she *is* rejecting you. In a way, she's a challenge. The mind is clever. It easily deceives us, and often makes us see love where there is only an obstacle to our will. Don't confuse love with the desire to possess someone mentally or physically. It's a common mistake, and the reason why so many relationships don't last.

'The mind is forever creating new desires. When one's satisfied, it dies, and another takes over. Have you ever wondered what would happen if she had said, "Yes"? Don't you think you would have said, "No. Wait!", stopped loving her that very instant, and started off again on your quest for love?'

Again, I was at a loss for words.

'Do you know why you're suffering?' Maitri asked. 'It's *not* because you love this woman. Love that comes from the heart, and not from the mind, real love, never causes suffering. In fact, it is the only source of true happiness. No. You're not suffering because you love her, you're suffering because you're asking her to love you.'

Maitri then suggested we leave the café and go for a walk. I willingly agreed. Being with her seemed to have such a calming effect on me. She did confuse me, it was true, but what she said unveiled new light.

It was a mild day. The sun was shining. Maitri walked very slowly, as if she had all the time in the world. I remembered something I'd wanted to ask her, but hadn't had the courage.

'What do you do? I mean, what work do you ...?'

She smiled, as though it were irrelevant.

'I'm travelling', she said.

'You don't live here?'

'No. I'm staying with some friends.'

'You still haven't told me what you do?'

'Let's just say that ... I teach.'

I felt it best not to insist. She seemed so evasive, reticent to talk about herself. Maybe she was hiding something. No, she was too direct. But there was something almost sacred about her, about everything she did, as though she were carrying out some mysterious ritual.

'You've already taken a big step', she said.

'What d'you mean?'

'By keeping a diary.'

I was taken aback. Had I mentioned it to her? I had the uneasy feeling she could read my mind, my innermost thoughts.

'You've already taken a big step', Maitri repeated, 'because the person who sees that ordinary love means suffering can also see how this suffering begins. The most common mistake we make is looking for happiness in someone else, instead of finding it in ourselves. Where else could we find it?'

'Does that mean we have to give up loving?'

'No. On the contrary, we come to Earth to learn how to love. And only when we've learned really to love everyone, all human beings, is our work here finished. When a man loves a woman, he's still just a beginner in the School of Love.

'He loves the members of his family, those close to him, eventually, after a very long time, all human beings. Each of us has a long way to go before we get to that point. But there's no rush, is there?'

Once more, her questions had caught me off-guard. After all the serious things she said, was she joking? I didn't have time to answer her.

'People are running all over the place looking for happiness. Looking for love. Everything would be so much easier if they just looked inside themselves, where the fountainhead of true love lies.'

We walked on in silence. We soon reached a park, and Maitri suggested we sit down for a while. She fascinated me, the way she spoke so eloquently of love. I asked her if she'd ever been married. She laughed again.

'No, never. But you, Leonard, tell me: do you

actually think you're going to marry her?'

'I hope so.'

'Tell me, why? Why do you want to?'

'I told you, 'cause I love her.'

'And you'll be happier when you're married?'

'Of course.'

'And what'll you do then?'

Maitri sure had a knack for twisting things.

'Well, I ... Well, to be honest, I don't know.'

'What good is wanting to be happy,' she asked, 'if you don't know what you'll do with it? Why want happiness, anyway? Aren't you just being selfish?'

Was she serious? Or just trying to provoke me? She didn't seem to be joking. I found her compassionate, tender.

'When I find happiness, I mean ... God! I feel foolish answering this ridiculous question. We all want it! That's all!'

'You're right,' Maitri said, 'the quest for happiness is what life's all about. Listen. You may not understand me now. But believe me:

> EACH MOMENT OF YOUR LIFE YOU HAVE AS MUCH REASON TO BE HAPPY AS UNHAPPY, WHATEVER THE CIRCUMSTANCES.

'So, there's absolutely nothing compelling you to hope for something in the future, or to delay for a single instant the moment when you can be perfectly happy.

'Understand what I mean?' she asked, then smiled.

'Sort of', I hesitantly replied.

'Let's take your life, for example, since that's the one you know best. Right now, you're free. You may feel alone because there is no one in your life, but solitude has its advantages, like any other state of being.

'You have your hopes up. You want to marry this woman. But how do you know you'll be happy together? Won't problems pop up? Won't you wind up like everyone else? You're bound to hit some snags in your relationship, should you, of course, have one.

'And the reason for it is, you live on the "mental" plane, or on "desire", not with the "heart". What prevents us from being happy is not being able to see how perfect any given situation is.

'Everything that happens to you has a reason. Nothing is left to chance. And do you know why you're *not* in tune with the perfect harmony in your

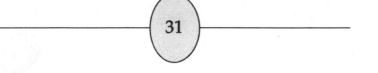
life? Why you don't see that what's happening between you and Susan *has to* happen?

'It's because you don't live in the present, in the here and now. You live in your mind, in what *you* desire. You don't see reality as it really is, so you can't appreciate its marvellous splendour.

'You're distracted away from the present, living in illusion. That's why you're miserable. When we aren't living in the present, we're living in hatred. We hate life. That might not be easy to understand, but think about it.

'When we live in the present, our masks come off. They no longer make sense, and our desires wither away like autumn leaves. Hatred towards others, just as hating oneself, is impossible.

'Transcend. Go beyond the illusion of time, put an end to the pursuit and the evasion that make up your reality, and you'll have the ultimate encounter of your life: the encounter with your real self.

'Then, and only then, you'll begin to love yourself. You'll love yourself and you'll understand the perfection of your life. Then you'll be able to live the Noble Life.

'Do you hear me? You're a fallen Master. You've forgotten your true nature. You're in self-imposed exile! You've lost your throne, your kingdom, and its riches. That's why you're so poor, a riches to rags story, a bum. Do you understand what I'm telling you?'

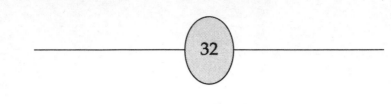

'More or less', I said. 'But if nothing happens by chance, if everything in life is perfect, how come my love life is a mess? And has caused me such misery? Shouldn't happiness be automatic? Even if love's weird? How come we can love someone who doesn't love us?'

'When you love someone, he or she loves you', said Maitri. 'That's the Law of Correspondence. And because that's true, it's impossible to think about someone who's not thinking about you. I can assure you that this Susan who is constantly on your mind is also thinking about you.'

'She may be thinking about me, but she certainly doesn't love me.'

Maitri reached into her jacket pocket and took out her little book. She opened it. 'Here's something interesting written by the spiritual Master, Peter Deunov:

IF YOU LOVE SOMEONE, HE LOVES YOU.

He already loves you in his soul and his Higher or Superior consciousness. But this love has not yet manifested in his Inferior consciousness, his ordinary, Earthly consciouness. It is written, 'As above, so below'. For this reason, the love which is above, in Higher consciousness, will eventually descend and be manifested on Earth to us.

But the person you love can only feel and welcome your love when the necessary conditions are present.

Imagine a man whose head and feet are held in a vice. How is he going to talk to you? How can he even hear you? In order for him to understand you, first you'll have to free his head and feet. Just as a damaged pitcher cannot hold water, so a damaged heart cannot hold love.

If love enters a heart that has cracks in it, it quickly seeps out. Love seeks out sturdy hearts, hearts that are strong. When someone complains that someone doesn't love them, that proves he is pouring his love into broken containers ... the love escapes at once. If the one you love is not ready, your love will not find an echo in him until much later.

I found his message comforting. It means that if I loved Susan, surely she loved me. I saw that the Law of Correspondence often played a part in my life, although it could take ages – from a year to ten – for the circle to be closed, to know requited love. But by then *my* love for *her* might have long since disappeared.

Why? Because I was no longer free? Because my heart now belonged to an Other? Because I'd changed and was as different as she was?

Or, perhaps, I'd never really loved *them*, even during the most ecstatic moments of passion. Because what I'd really wanted, secretly, ironically, was for them to reject me? Because long ago, I'd been rejected by another woman, namely, mother, and I could only try to exorcise this age-old pain by repeating it again and again?

But wasn't there something to learn from all this bad timing? That life is a never-ending course in self-renunciation? And when we have any problem whatsoever licked, it just vanishes, as if by magic? As if some arcane law were at work?

'A man', Maitri continued, 'should never ask a woman if she loves him. By doing that, he restrains her. And love can only blossom in freedom. So, it is better to remain silent.'

She closed her little book. She sat there perfectly still, which gave me time to think. I couldn't help but wonder if I hadn't irrevocably alienated Susan.

Maitri had taught me a great deal, but one thing still bothered me.

'You said there is a reason for everything. Alright. Susan isn't ready, but why did I meet the very woman who isn't available? Wouldn't it have been much simpler if I'd met someone else who was?'

'Whatever the case,

WE ALWAYS MEET OURSELF.

'When we face difficulties, we should look for the cause inside ourselves. Everything must be brought back to the self. People always behave towards us the way we act towards them. Others are a perfect mirror.'

'C'mon', I said. 'What did I do wrong? I loved her!'

'Come,' Maitri said, getting up, 'you'll understand. Let's go to my place.'

I didn't say 'No'. But this was the most unexpected

move of hers yet. We walked from the park to her place. Maitri didn't say anything, and I was too nervous to open my mouth. She stopped in front of a very large, rather quaint Tudor-style mansion.

'Here we are', she said, and led me in.

The rooms were enormous, but sparsely furnished. A few pieces here and there, at most. Some unusual curios. But the house didn't seem empty.

Maitri invited me into the living-room, and I sat down on an elegant sofa. She excused herself, put a record on and left. Left alone, I began to feel a little uneasy. The music was oriental. I heard the delicate, tinkling sounds of many tiny bells that seemed to be calling a long-lost traveller.

Then came a flute, soft and mysterious, accompanied by an unusual instrument I'd never heard before. Tears suddenly trickled down my face. I don't know why. It was so strange. I'd almost forgotten. Now, listening to the music, I remembered, 'I have a soul!' Just then, Maitri came back with two fine, little teacups on a tray. She sat next to me on the sofa.

'Now, you can understand why Susan is taking so long to love you, and why your paths were meant to cross. You've got to settle things.'

She focused her compelling eyes on mine, as if to hypnotise me. 'Take the cup. And now drink it. Don't be afraid. I promise you, it won't do you any harm.'

I wanted to refuse. But I couldn't put the cup down. I suddenly became suspicious of her. I wondered if Maitri, in spite of her dignified air, really had some evil design on me. Was she trying to poison me?

'Are you having any?' I asked her.

Smiling, she drank her tea. Then she looked at me to see if I was reassured, confirming my belief that she could read my mind. Now, I had no choice. I sipped my tea.

The tea was exquisite and delicately flavoured. I felt relieved, but my relief was premature. As soon as I put my cup down, I lost consciousness. Or, I seemed to be swept away in an altered state of consciousness, though I still knew what was going on.

It was as if I were day-dreaming, and every detail of what I saw was incredibly clear. I was in a big house or a castle of long ago, perhaps the thirteenth or fourteenth century. Not being up on my history, I can't say for sure. But whoever lived there was extremely wealthy and lived in the lap of luxury. I was in an enormous living-room that was like a cathedral full of light.

I wasn't alone. There was a woman standing near a window. I couldn't see her face. Her back was to me. She was wearing a long, very elegant gown. Near her on the table was a beautiful leather-bound edition of Dante's *Divine Comedy*. And beside it was a manuscript, the title of which was *The Canterbury Tales*. When I saw the books, I was strangely moved, as if they brought back some memory. A bit of *déjà vu*.

When I heard the woman's voice, I immediately recognised it. She spoke in Middle English, but I had no difficulty in understanding her.

'Geoffrey, why don't you just admit it? You don't love me and you never intended to marry me.'

Who's Geoffrey? But it seemed perfectly natural to answer her. Walking up to her, I saw myself in the mirror. Oh, my God! It can't be! I have another body! Don't tell me, I was someone else!

'Give me time,' I said, 'my duties as Counsellor are very demanding.'

'I've been waiting for almost a year!'

'Be patient. Philippa, you know I love you.'

Who? Why had I called her that? Philippa? Where did I get that from? From what recesses of the mind? What an awful name!

She didn't say anything. I felt uneasy, as guilty as sin. What didn't I want to tell her? Why wasn't I being honest with her?

'There's another woman, isn't there?' she demanded.

God! I had a mistress! What was I to do? This might destroy my future.

'I assure you, there's no one else.'

She said nothing. Dreaming is different from being awake, and plays by its own rules. Philippa turned to face me. She was strikingly beautiful! Long blonde curls swept around that face and those incredible green eyes.

I heard Susan's voice and, suddenly, I understood everything! I went up to Philippa, grabbed her by the shoulders, and looking right into her eyes, I demanded, 'Who are you?' I guess I shook her up.

'It's me, Philippa', she said, astonished by what I'd just done. 'Geoffrey, are you alright?'

'Fine. But there's something strange going on here. Philippa, we're in a dream.'

'What are you talking about?' she wanted to know.

Thinking I was ill, she caressed my forehead and asked, 'My love, are you sure you don't have a fever?'

'You're not who you think you are!' I shouted at her. 'And I'm not who you think I am either!'

I was exasperated by this bizarre turn of events, and, almost begging, I asked her, 'I'm Leonard. Don't you recognise me?'

'Enough is enough! Now Geoffrey, stop it!'

'No, no! You don't understand!'

I held her in my arms.

'Look into my eyes. Think very hard. Go back ... back. You're not Philippa. This is just a dream. Wake up, or we'll never be able to love one another!'

She undoubtedly thought I'd gone mad.

'Please, Geoffrey. Stop!' she cried. 'For God's sake!'

I realised it was no use. Philippa couldn't comprehend what I was trying to say. She'd have to be having the same dream to do that. I let her go. We stood there, facing one another. She managed a smile.

'Geoffrey, never mind. I have a gift for you.'
'A gift?'
'Yes, surprised? Wait here. I'll get it!'
She disappeared into the next room and returned moments later, holding a box wrapped in lovely blue velvet. She held it out to me.

I took it and quickly opened it. Inside was a magnificent bracelet, set with green stones.
'It's beautiful', I said, 'thank you.'
But I didn't really like it, and she knew I was lying.
'You don't like it?'
'Of course, I do. On my word of honour, I adore it.'

But in fact, I was upset. Because at that very moment I remembered the bracelet with green gems I had given to Susan. Was this why my gift had had so little effect on her? I obviously wasn't convincing enough.
'Never mind', she sighed.
Then she got out some red wine and poured us

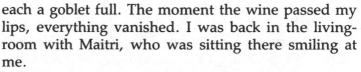

each a goblet full. The moment the wine passed my lips, everything vanished. I was back in the living-room with Maitri, who was sitting there smiling at me.

'Whoa! My head! What happened? Where was I? Oh! I remember.' On the table in front of me was my tea, still hot and steamy. So, I couldn't have been gone for more than a minute or two. I looked at Maitri.

'Are you a witch? A sorceress?'

'Yes, if you like.'

'Casting spells? But how did you do that?'

'Not now. You'll have to wait. When you love, you'll know. You'll be given great powers.'

'But ...?'

'I made you search in the archives of your memory, where the files of your countless past lives are. I wanted you to understand why you're having such problems with Susan.'

'So, I was right. Philippa was Susan!'

'Life is an enormous vessel filled with water', Maitri continued. 'The stone I drop into the vessel makes concentric circles that ripple out to its walls, then invariably return to where they began. Man is in the centre of the vessel.

EACH THOUGHT, EACH ACTION PRODUCES A CIRCLE WHICH INEVITABLY COMES BACK.

'People don't always understand or respect this truth. Sometimes, because of this it takes a very long time to come full circle.

'It may take many lifetimes before all the circumstances are present and things materialise. That's why some people feel that life has treated them unfairly, while others believe they can do evil things with impunity.'

She paused momentarily, then continued.

'In reality, there's no injustice. All suffering is the result of past errors, often forgotten because they were made in a previous lifetime. We make mistakes because we don't know enough, and sooner or later we have to pay for it.

'What's the difference between a wise man and an ordinary man? If the wise man is happy, it's because he understands. He understands, namely, that his actions have consequences, and so he acts in a way that always creates goodness around him. Thus, what inevitably comes back to him is happiness.

'Romantic relationships are no exception to this Law of Returns. In your case, for example, if Susan appears so hesitant, so ambivalent, it's because you behaved that way towards her in another lifetime.

'Remember ...

'Long ago, in England, you two were together. In fact, you have been following each other for centuries. You were together in Upper Egypt. She was a temple priestess. You were a person of great authority. You were not married during that incarnation, but you were very closely bound. You have accomplished great things together.

'During your incarnation in medieval England, however, you caused Susan a great deal of suffering. Today, she is paying you back, so to speak. She doesn't know it. It happened so long ago.

'She was a very high soul, and had developed great powers in previous incarnations, especially when she was a priestess in ancient Egypt.

'But because she didn't always use those powers in accordance with the Law of Love, she lost them. You also had a similar fall from grace and lost the powers you had acquired a long time ago.

'But things will soon change, for both of you. You are beginning to understand. It usually takes time, even hundreds of lifetimes. This understanding doesn't usually come before most of our past debts have been settled. If it were not so, the Principle of Retribution would not be respected.

'So take heart, for these revelations mean you will soon know happiness. They come to you now because the fruits of your spirit are ripe.

'I know you have endured much in this life. But during your incarnation in England your high rank as well as your charm allowed you to abuse the trust of several women. That is why, in your present life, your love for several women has been unrequited.

'The Masters that guide your destiny and enable

you to become free have chosen to let you experience all this suffering, and atone for your previous mistakes in the space of twelve years, which are now coming to an end.'

What Maitri had been saying was so astounding that for a moment I was afraid I'd go mad. I felt as though the secret doors I shouldn't have access to had been opened for me. Is that why we – souls in metempsychosis – forget our previous incarnations?

It was as if Maitri had told me as much as I could handle. She had stretched me to the limit. And incredible as her words seemed, she had spoken with such certainty that I didn't doubt her for a second.

'I have released your memory of previous lives so you can place greater trust in what I tell you', she said.

'But how,' I asked her, 'can I know when I am making a mistake? A mistake I could avoid?'

'I've already told you. Simply act in accordance with the Law of Love.

FOR EACH THOUGHT, EACH WORD, EACH ACT, ASK YOURSELF:
AM I DOING THIS OUT OF LOVE OR POWER?

'And how do we know whether we're acting out of love and not power? Our inner voice always tells us, if we choose to listen.

'We can also ask ourselves: "Am I helping her?

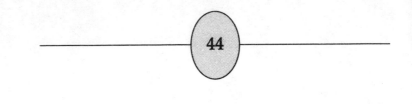

Would I want her to do the same thing to me? Would I treat my mother, or my sister or my daughter the same way? What would the Master do? Would he do the same thing?"

'Ignorance prevents us from realising that:

WHAT WE DO TO OTHERS, WE DO TO OURSELVES.

'Always remember, the power-hungry man who abuses others abuses himself. And, in the end, without understanding why, he winds up empty-handed. But the man who gives all he has will inherit a treasure so great it is unimaginable. Because the more you give, the more you shall receive. It is a universal law which suffers no exception.

'Jesus said: "Love thy neighbour as thou wouldst love thyself."

'Most people don't know that before we can love others we must love ourselves. This doesn't mean selfish love, which is just a mask for the self-hatred that motivates so many.

'In the sublime *Bhagavad-Gita* it is written:

> By one's Self should one raise oneself, and not allow oneself to sink; for Self alone is the friend of the self, and Self alone is the self's foe.

'Each time someone goes against spiritual laws he is acting as his own enemy. But when he respects this, he is learning to become his best and everyone's best friend.

'When we have learned to live by such love, our stay here is completed, and we are ready to evolve toward other realms, where other far greater tasks, greater than our present understanding can even imagine, await us.'

I take the liberty here of jumping ahead in my account. Later that same evening, I thought about what Maitri had said concerning my problems in matters of the heart, and I felt drawn to a particular book in my library, Raymond Bernard's *Messages from the Celestial Sanctum*.

Now, think what you will about bibliomancy, that science that supposedly allows you to foresee your future by opening a book at random. The fact remains that by a coincidence so striking it tempts one to believe there is no such thing as pure chance, and that everything in our lives is significant, I opened the book at the following passage, whose relevance greatly impressed me:

> The mystic seeks again the significance and lesson of all circumstances, good or not, which constitute the plot of his life, knowing that they will cease as soon as they have been understood and assimilated, bringing him closer to the goal, to a greater grasp of consciousness.

So, each situation in life has something to teach us.

Suffering offers us not only a key, but also the hope that we will become free. It is a stairway to heaven.

The fact that I had met Maitri who had introduced me to this philosophy, and had happened upon this passage, was probably because I was at a turning-point in my life. And the same applies to the reader of this page who understands it, and accepts it as true.

Further on in the passage, Bernard writes:

> ... if advancing along the path the knowledge acquired does not lead him to better behaviour, it is evident that he will be more guilty than the ignorant. And the lesson to be learned will be more difficult, even though the capacity for voluntary redress may be allowed if he wishes to use it in time.
>
> On the other hand, if his sincerity is great, if the steps along the Path lead him to just thoughts and actions, he will naturally have less difficulty in understanding the effects of his past karma, favourable or not, and the law will soften and shorten the situations from which a lesson must be learned.
>
> In some cases the karmic effects will even be

annulled if acquired evolution makes useless an experience which provides nothing more to the interior development. In particular, whoever would have developed true love in himself, to the point where all his thoughts and actions would be impreg nated by it, would only be little or not at all subject to the karmic law in its negative phase. His life would be harmonious and the ultimate return established or very nearly so.

I end my digression here, and return to my account once again.

In her mellifluous voice, Maitri continued. 'In the *Bhagavad-Gita* we also find wisdom as subtle as this:

> Abiding always in the eternal truth, scorn to gain or guard anything. Be your own Master.

'What does this tell us? What is the eternal truth? It is the state man attains when the flame of love burns in his heart. And what is it to be your own Master? It is to live freely, in the continuous flow of love, detached, for such is the true nature of man, even though he lives everywhere in chains.

'The moment we cease to love, the moment we become attached to someone or something, we cease to be ourselves, and we are unhappy. When you begin to truly love, when you become one with the Sublime Thought and live the Noble Life, you will feel an inner sun shining in your heart. Within you will be the Endless Summer. From that moment on, darkness and shadows will disappear from your life.

'So learn to cultivate this love which alone can enable you to rise above life's contradictions. Abide always in the eternal truth, scorn to gain or guard anything. Be the Master of yourself. Do you understand what I mean?'

'I'm not quite sure', I admitted. 'The way you talk, you seem to be against love, as we ordinarily know it.'

'I'm not against love *per se*. I'm only trying to show you that love can be an illusion. Remember, anyone who seeks someone else's love is doomed to unhappiness.

'Love must be a gift, an opening up.

WHEN LOVE MEANS ATTACHMENT, IT LEADS TO SUFFERING.

'So, I repeat, I'm not against love. I am merely trying to explain how suffering starts, and how to put an end to it, so that anyone who is tired of suffering can be set free.'

'What about marriage?' I asked her.

'Marriage is only natural for souls on this planet. Celibacy is not recommended. Only some can handle it. Most incarnated souls have scores to settle together which could not be accomplished in the celibate state.

'Human love is a great school for wisdom and

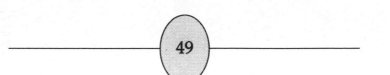

nobility. But just as the body must be seen as the temple of the spirit and not a plaything for the senses, marriage and human love must be seen as the noble union of two souls for spiritual purposes.

'It takes lovers a long time to discover that ultimately they are but two souls on a transitional voyage, in this vessel we call the body. If the souls are not united from the start, it will not be long before the bodies drift apart, because genuine marriage is primarily a union of two souls.

'How great is the sadness of those lovers who realise their error. They have profaned their love, as the temple was profaned. They are strangers. They have forgotten that, first and foremost, they have souls. They *are* souls!

'So from now on, begin to cultivate real love, which alone can enable you to rise above life's contradictions. That is why we can say:

WHEN THERE IS CONTRADICTION, THERE IS NO LOVE.
WHEN THERE IS LOVE, THERE IS NO CONTRADICTION.

'Look within yourself. Concern yourself with the part of your being that is real, what the seers of all ages have called the self, or high self.'

Maitri smiled.

'Just as Jesus said that there are many rooms in his Father's house, so there are many keys that will open the door to the higher self. There is a very simple one

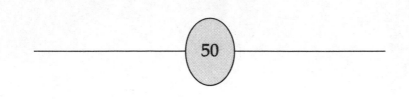

that has allowed many wise men to obtain liberation. It is meditation, concentrating on a mantra, a very powerful word which helps awaken the hidden energy in everyone.

'The mantra I'm going to give you comes from the very ancient Siddhas, enlightened beings who have transcended the limits of the human condition and live in a state of perfect bliss. The mantra is:

OM NAMAH SHIVAYA.

It means:

I BOW BEFORE MYSELF, I CONTEMPLATE MYSELF.

'It is said that we become what we contemplate. By contemplating our higher self and mentally repeating our mantra, we rise above our lower self and realise our true nature. So meditate every day. Begin with half an hour in the morning, and half an hour in the evening. Then gradually meditate a little longer each day.

'But I warn you, it's not as easy as it sounds. The mind is inattentive and unruly by nature. After a few minutes, even a few seconds, it starts to wander off. You'll think of other things. You'll feel a tremendous resistance.

'You may wonder why you're sitting there in your room, repeating this mantra. Being sceptical, doubt-

ful about it, is only normal. You'll have to struggle
with it.

'You'll also have to overcome a very great fear, the
fear of death. You're really not afraid of death. But
the false self, the limited narrow self, the Ego, is. And
the Ego will fight, and do anything to survive.

'Like a true hero, your valour will be tested. You're
waging the most important battle of your life – a
battle for your life!

'The history of mankind repeats itself again and
again, and behind all the different masks, each
individual drama is the same. You are the knight of
all the legends. The dragon is your lower self, and the
mantra is the sword you will use to slay it.

'Like Ulysses in Homer's *The Odyssey*, you'll meet
countless obstacles on the voyage you'll make to find
your true homeland. Persevere. Every step you take,
no matter how small, is important. It takes a lifetime
to reach the highest level of meditation.

'Gradually, because of your devotion, you'll come
to understand everything I've told you. For meditation releases the true inner wisdom that even the
most profound books can only allude to.

'I could talk to you for hours about the mantra's
power. Whole treatises have been written about it.
But very often, theory just satisfies our curiosity and
distracts us from our main purpose: the discovery of
the secret door to freedom.

'A single minute of meditation is worth more than

ten hours of discussion. If the remedy works, use it. How can we feel the benefits of a magic elixir if we refuse to take it?

'Today, I offer you the sublime chalice of meditation. I urge you not to reject it. Drink from it, and satisfy at last your age-old thirst for a new life, free from all fear, hatred and weariness.'

I started to ask Maitri many questions, but she brushed them aside, saying, 'Didn't you understand what I just said?' I blushed, with embarrassment. As if to spare me further discomfort, she went on, patiently.

'One day when the Buddha was in a forest, he took some leaves in his hand and asked the Bhikkus, the mendicant monks who were with him: "What do you think, O Bikkhus? Which is more? These leaves in my hand, or the leaves in the forest?"

'"Master, very few are the leaves in the hand of the Blessed One, but the leaves in the forest are abundant", was their answer.

'"Even so, Bikkhus, of what I have known I have told you only a little, and what I have not told you is far more. And why have I not told you more? Because it is not useful ... It does lead to Nirvana. That is why."

'It is the same with the mantra', continued Maitri.

'Don't trouble your mind with useless questions. Take my word for it. I can tell you this – if I had to die tomorrow and I could say just one more thing, this is

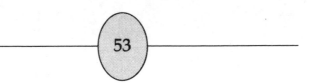

what I would leave to you as my legacy. Repeat the mantra:

OM NAMAH SHIVAYA.

'This is the true music of life. All the rest, the poet said, is only words.

'Through meditation you'll begin to live the Noble Life, from which springs peace and happiness. You'll become a perfect circle. You'll become your own fulfilment, both cause and effect.'

'But how can I apply this to my romantic relationships?' I asked.

'Easily. Passion is both selfish and limiting, because it seeks only its own gratification. In true love, your isolation ends, and suffering with it.

'Too many people shut themselves off from love because they were once disappointed. They believe that if they suffered once, they will inevitably suffer again. They still live in the past and cherish the scars of their old wounds, so they always hide behind a mask. They never see the real face of those they meet, because they quickly cover it with the distorting veil of their fears and dreams.

'How many people do you know who are open to a new experience?' Maitri continued. 'Very few. In fact, people are blinded by their passions and by the feeling that they have a separate existence from others. They are blinded by their Ego. They are mistaken when they believe they are different from others, and limit themselves by not being open.

'Look at most people. They're pathetically closed because they live by hate, without realising it. When we live by the principle of love, we are open to others.

'That's a subtle and incomprehensible paradox for anyone who hasn't experienced it but:

> BY OPENING UP COMPLETELY TO OTHERS, WE ARE NO LONGER DEPENDENT UPON THEM.

'In a way we become like a child who feels immense joy when he is with someone, but doesn't miss him when he is gone – simply because he lives totally absorbed in the moment, happily playing.

'What's more, since he lives in the present, in a sense the child has no Ego, or at least no consciousness of his own existence.

'It's Ego-awareness that separates us from the "now" and that causes us to feel alone.

> THE PERSON WHO LIVES IN THE PERFECT PRESENT NEVER SUFFERS FROM LONELINESS.

'However, we can say of him that he lives in true solitude, which in fact is the very absence of "aloneness".

'That's why the person who lives on the "heart"

plane never misses anyone. How could he? He's no longer conscious of his lower self which is precisely the cause of suffering! At the same time, each experience becomes a marvellous celebration. The veil between him and others no longer exists.

'He sees others as they are, and seeing them as they are, he loves them.'

'Why?' I asked.

'It may seem mystifying, but being present in the moment implies the death of the Ego: the individual fits perfectly into any given situation, everything happens spontaneously, giving rise to love. The current that springs forth from meditation and the current that springs forth from love are one and the same.'

Maitri smiled, as usual. She seemed to be enjoying every minute of this. It was as if she had all the time in the world. She possessed the great gift that she could give freely to an Other, even to a stranger, as if he were an old friend, as if he were a brother she was seeing again after a long separation, or just before a long journey.

That's what I found so attractive about Maitri – her charming 'availability', her presence. I couldn't help but compare it with the unavailability of other women, those I'd loved or thought I had.

And what about 'availability'?

Had I been open to women? To their splendour, their hopes and dreams? No. I'd often been bored after a couple of minutes with them. I'd half-listened, little interested in the secrets that they, having trusted me, confided.

It was only before making love, when I passionately wanted them, that I'd ever felt close to them, or attentive – with an attention that was nonetheless obviously egotistical.

To be honest, in my whole life I'd never truly 'met' anyone, which was why I was so unhappy, and so drawn to Maitri. Her not having an Ego created a kind of 'emptiness', and it was this that made her so fascinating.

She virtually never talked to me about herself, perhaps because this almost inevitably meant talking about her past, 'the' past, about what one was, what one had been.

Maitri said, 'Real generosity means giving whatever you have. Give without asking yourself, "Am I making a mistake? Am I a fool for believing in Others? To whom should I be open?"

'Again I say, "Give!" And if they're not ready, they will not receive. If, on the other hand, they are ready, they will benefit. But it is not for you to decide.

'A great author wrote, "What I spent, I had. What I kept, I lost. What I give, I *have*."

'Everyone should be as generous,' Maitri said, 'but their Egos get in the way. Their Egos maintain the illusion that by closing themselves off, by not giving of themselves, they will hold onto whatever they have, when, in reality, they have nothing.

'For as I've told you, the more we give, the more we receive. But don't confuse real generosity with ordinary generosity, which always expects something in return. Some people don't really give, they merely trade.

'When they give, they're saying, "What will you give me in return?" They're expecting something. And because they are selfish, they suffer and are disappointed.

'Those motivated by goodness never complain. Being well motivated means living in peace.

'He who lives a perfect existence is one who acts out of love, without Ego, and never complains. How could he? There's no one left to complain!'

As she spoke these last words, Maitri started laughing. But this was no ordinary laugh. It was a mad, all-consuming laughter she seemed unable to control.

'Who could complain?' she repeated. 'There's not

even anyone left to complain to. The place is empty. In fact, it's always been empty. The Ego does not exist!'

Her joy became mine. I didn't understand everything she was telling me, probably not even a fraction of it, but a feeling of freedom welled up in me.

This woman was so beautiful, so free-spirited, yet able to converse on such a profound metaphysical level. And I'd thought that the love she spoke about required a joyless renunciation, a dreary life without passion!

Watching her I realised how frightfully seriously I'd been taking myself all these years, perhaps all my life, while mistakenly believing I'd been fairly easy-going.

Maitri regained her composure and apologised. I assured her that I was delighted to see her this way, that she was radiant, and that her surprising gaiety had changed everything, everything I'd believed up to then about mystics. It was the first time I'd used the word 'mystic', and it had spontaneously come to my mind. I was convinced of it: Maitri was a mystic!

She said: 'The world mirrors our heart!'

She had suddenly become serious again, almost solemn. It was a characteristic of hers that amazed me, this unique ability to slip effortlessly and unexpectedly from one state to another. One moment, she was as happy as can be; the next, as serious. Perhaps it was merely because, inwardly, she was always the same, and simply projected different exteriors in some magical way.

'People spend hours looking for someone to love, going to cafés ...'

She smiled as she said this, as though teasing me because, after all, we'd met in a café.

'They go to restaurants, to theatres, when all they really have to do is open themselves up. Someone who is truly open and accessible doesn't have to look for love.

'People are attracted to those in whom love has begun to flow.

IF YOU WANT TO BE LOVED, YOU MUST START BY LOVING.

'When we are at peace with ourselves, when we are our own best friend, we attract the very people we need for our fulfilment.

'And because we immediately are drawn to them, without any expectations, the encounter is genuine. But when we have some particular romantic ideal in mind, we never meet anyone who can live up to it, and we're almost always disappointed.

'But there's another even more profound and more subtle way to know perfect love.

'One day the Buddha said to his disciples:

O Bhikkus, 'I may not be, I may not have', this idea is frightening to the uninstructed worldling.

'Similarly, the idea of giving up ordinary love, of expecting nothing from the Other, of no longer being one who loves, no longer possessing the Other, or belonging to the Other, can also be frightening.

'But it is frightening because we misunderstand perfect love. Only the person willing to completely surrender his "I", his Ego, and no longer wishing to possess the Other, can discover love's splendour. Such a highly attuned person will meet the perfect mate, if that is his destiny.

'But he will no longer suffer from not being with him. He will be totally committed to unselfishly serving others, so he wouldn't ask anything for himself. And who after all is he to demand anything? Demanding something would mean that he was still suffering.

'The person who transcends the primitive, yet widespread, notion that he "exists", is fulfilled. If he has a wife, he will accept her and welcome her with love and respect, fully aware of the sacred nature of their marriage, and of the journey they will take together.

'So believe me, this is the time to adopt the philosophy of love. Demystify yourself and know your true nature. Live the Noble Life.'

Maitri became silent and withdrew into herself. Had she said everything she had to? Her eyes were closed. I felt it was a sign for me to go. Then she opened her eyes. I thanked her for her hospitality, even though I wasn't sure why I was leaving, and actually hadn't the slightest desire to do so. Had Maitri made that decision for me?

But there was still a crucial question troubling me. Of course, it concerned the woman I was so deeply in love with.

'What should I do about Susan?' I asked.

'Close all the doors of your senses', she said. 'Become a eunuch, for a while. Your desire for her is still not pure, no matter what you say.'

'Is that all I have to do?'

'It's much more of a trial than you think. Until now, desire has brought you women. You're like a wild stallion. That's why you feel so deprived. From now on, desire must grow out of your love. Let your desire become like a woman's, with your love coming before your lust.

'You must find your centre again, your true domain. You can do this through your heart, but never through desire. Desire is but one of hate's faces. Follow after it and you will only come to dwell in the Outer Darkness.'

She had hit the bull's-eye, the reason for my unhappy love life. But I had to ask her: 'Do you think that Susan loves me? That we'll be together one day?'

'Have you forgotten so soon?

IF YOU DOUBT THE OTHER'S LOVE, YOUR OWN LOVE IS IN DOUBT.

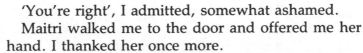

'You're right', I admitted, somewhat ashamed.

Maitri walked me to the door and offered me her hand. I thanked her once more.

'Will we see each other again?' I asked.

'Yes. One more time.'

'When?'

'When the time comes.'

I didn't attempt to set a specific time. On my way out, undoubtedly to reassure me because I appeared troubled, she said, 'Do nothing else. Be happy. She will come.'

On that note, I left her. Back home, I lay on my bed and thought for hours about what she'd said. I kept hearing her say, 'Do nothing else. Be happy. She will come.'

At the time, I didn't realise how hard it would be to follow such advice. Or how subtle and profound it was.

'Do nothing else.' Don't try to see Susan any more. Don't write or phone her any more. Instead, leave things alone. Let silence, mysterious and powerful, do its work. Love in silence. And from a distance. Be confident. Love her.

Love her? If I sincerely love her, she surely loves me too, and sooner or later, our love will be fulfilled.

But when? Would I have the patience to wait? The strength to hold out? Or was this just a lot of hocus pocus? How come it's so difficult to follow these universal laws?

How come most people in love aren't happy? Aren't all love affairs just a nuisance? And when they manage to survive aren't they doomed to a perpetual grinding tedium, a sort of death?

'Do nothing else. Be happy.' Perhaps I could put Part One of her advice into action. After all, it shouldn't be impossible to do nothing for a while.

But being rather impulsive and impatient by nature, well ... Alright, it might be just as easy to wait, without dreaming about *her*. For years now, I'd been unable to spend a single week-end without female companionship.

Oh. 'Be happy', she said. It wasn't easy. In fact, it might be impossible. 'Be happy.' Ha! That's a laugh! What is happiness? Huh? It's so elusive and unpredictable. As soon as you've got it, it's gone.

And if I understand her correctly, I'd have to be happy without Susan. In fact, it was a prerequisite for her coming back. To be happy without her, even though I was absolutely convinced I could only be happy with her: surely this was a contradiction, if not a mission impossible?

I wasn't in the habit of considering such questions seriously, which was perhaps the very reason why my life was such a mess. 'Be happy.' Sure.

Maitri's whole philosophy was contained in this one message. If I could somehow manage to be happy while continuing to love Susan without her loving me, I'd attain the here and now.

And if I could just transcend it all, I'd have no expectations. Then I'd understand why this woman was running away from me, offering me nothing but indifference. And I could accept her rejection and leave her without feeling bitter. All this was implied, it seemed, in her advice: 'Be happy'.

The irony of it all was that if I came to live by these principles, I'd be happy no matter what. Whether Susan came or didn't come, was there or wasn't there. Was Maitri playing games with me?

Did she know that we'd never be a couple, never be as one, and to spare me this disappointment, she had simply urged me to be happy, knowing it would inevitably free me from a love that was eating away at me, gnawing at my happiness? How could I know?

In spite of my confusion, there was something enlightening about this whole situation. Until my meeting with Susan, as a result of so many disappointments, I no longer believed there was a woman I could really love. Now I understood that it was only because I had yet to meet the right woman.

Sad thoughts crossed my mind. What if I had not met Susan? And if I hadn't 'recognised' her? That would have been the case without the sound advice of Maitri ... Maybe we can come across this 'one and only' woman, not even 'see' her, and continue on our way – because we're already 'involved', because we have still not lived out all the suffering we must pass through with women who are *not* the right one.

What prevents us from recognising our soul-mate, our true love, undoubtedly proves the greatest tragedy in our lives. Maybe we don't have to worry about it. From a mathematical point of view, if there is only one out there who can fit us perfectly, there is very little chance, if any, that we are going to meet. But life is bigger than we think, and the really important events of our love-life probably take place without us knowing it, because the fabric of our destiny is woven by invisible hands ...

Weeks went by. In spite of all my resolutions, I tried several times to contact Susan. Each time, she said, 'No'. Needless to say, it was discouraging.

To ease my pain, I tried to convince myself that I really didn't have that much in common with her. When we think we are so much like the Other, share the same hopes and dreams, isn't it just because our lenses are all fogged up? Because our love concentrates far too long on one particular facet of *her* total personality?

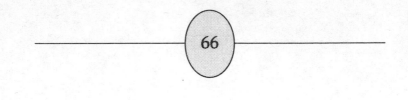

So, we leave unexamined equally important aspects that will eventually arouse the interest and fascination of another person, one who may appreciate them more.

I suddenly realised that my love for this woman was perhaps as unrealistic as my dream of becoming a writer in spite of the fact that no one reads my books.

And it occurred to me that just as it was perhaps time to step into line, and stop relying on the indulgence of wealthy friends and patrons to support my literary pretensions, so it was also perhaps time to let go of my senseless infatuation with Susan. In short, there were two fundamental facts I had to face:

1. I had no talent whatsoever.
2. This woman didn't love me.

Then one day, when my sense of hopelessness was at its worst, I received a letter from Maitri. It was totally unexpected, especially since I'd never given her my address. I quickly read it.

The letter couldn't have been more a propos. Coincidences seemed to be a trade mark of this inscrutable woman. It read:

> The impermanence of love is a warning. Look at all your past affairs and see how they died, one after the other. Life is brief, my friend. Life is very brief. Aren't you worn out? Haven't you suffered enough?

Think no more of this woman you love. Her refusal causes you such misery because you don't love her as you should. Be sincere. Bind the ties of the heart first.

Your heart is still not pure. You're not being totally honest with yourself. You've always turned love away, by running after those who didn't love you. But as I told you, this had to happen during the stage of purification that you are passing through and of which you're not aware. These women who have caused you such grief have suffered through you in the past. But you've nearly cleared it up. All this is nearly behind you.

And now you are ready to know perfect love. But first, you must come to the Temple. Knock on the door.

I can show you the Way, but I cannot travel the road for you. What good is the victory you've not won by yourself?

The happiness of ordinary love is nothing, a mere trifle compared with what awaits you. Learn how to die. Your Ego isn't holding you back. *You*'re holding onto it! Turn your heart and mind toward another ideal. Remember: we become what we contemplate.

Heed the words of the Master: 'Instead, seek his Kingdom, and all these things shall be yours.'

Stop trying to be what you are not. And in so doing, become what you are! Do you understand what I'm saying?

And so her letter ended. I read it over again. I'm not sure why, but this letter, in its simplicity, deeply touched me – so deeply, tears came to my eyes. What was it about this woman, that she could trouble me so much? I felt as though through her a distant voice were calling me. A voice that I'd always known, that I recognised, but had long forgotten – the voice of my very own soul.

Now I understood why I was sad, and why tears trickled down my face. It wasn't because I'd failed to win Susan's love, not even because of my failure as a writer. It was, in fact, because a new light was shining in my heart, and because suddenly my whole life seemed absurd.

Absurd because everything I'd done up until then – what did it amount to? Not much. In fact, nothing. Nothing but a series of ludicrous cravings and mediocre gratifications.

But now, faintly, intuitively, that distant voice was telling me: 'Life isn't what you think it is. Be courageous or your disenchantment will never end. To gain a glimpse of the cause of your misfortune and not take the crucial step forward will bring you even more misfortune.

'So, be brave! Have the courage to become what you are! Cast aside all social prejudices, your education, your old habits. They have all led you nowhere. They will lead to nothing in the future. You have discovered an eternal law. You need no more proof, for you have reached the very point where you perceive its truth, after centuries of illusion and disillusionment. The veil is now torn off. Why wait to enter the Temple? I tell you again and again:

HAVE THE COURAGE TO BECOME WHAT YOU ARE!

I tried as best as I could to make sense of this simple, yet mysterious message. It had not only awakened my thoughts, but also the wish to see Maitri again.

Hadn't she said we would meet one more time? Why only once more? Was she going somewhere or was she going to disappear? Was she going to die? Or had she merely said this to dramatise the situation? I didn't have her telephone number, or any way to contact her.

The day after I'd received her letter, I decided to go back to her place. It was an impulse I couldn't resist. I didn't really stop to consider whether or not she would see me.

It was just before noon when I got there, and I

wondered about inviting her to lunch. Just as I was going to knock, I had the most unusual feeling. Suddenly, there was poetry in my heart, and I felt as though I were about to meet my destiny.

Something important was going to happen. Something momentous, even holy, as ludicrous as that may sound. At the same time, I was very nervous. In a way, I felt that I was in danger, that I was going to die and, at the same time, going to start a new life.

I became so nervous that I wondered if I shouldn't leave. No doubt it was the anticipation of a major change. I suddenly held back, as we sometimes do when we confront an overpowering love, a love that feels too strong, too overwhelming. We choose to say 'never mind' and go on our way.

And we realise, too late, that out of sheer cowardice we've missed something special. Wasn't that exactly what I wanted? What I was about to do was ...

At times like this, we always find so many reasons for doing nothing, and a flurry of excuses came to mind. Maybe I was being inconsiderate? Maybe I'd be bothering her?

After all, I didn't really know Maitri. Perhaps, she'd consider me too forward, and would hardly appreciate such familiarity. I almost turned around and walked away, but something in me overcame my cowardice. Finally, I knocked, trembling with the secret feeling that I was on the verge of the most important meeting of my life!

Maitri opened the door. She greeted me with her enigmatic smile, and said, 'You're late.'

Was she joking? Was she trying to provoke me? Or was she simply showing me that her mind functioned on such a high plane that I was totally unaware of her meaning? She was not one to play games. But how could I tell if she was playing one, and playing it to the utmost?

She showed me in, then asked, 'Did you get my letter?'

'Yes.'

'Tell me what I said.'

As simply as her request was, she caught me off-guard. I stood there unable to speak.

'It appears you've remembered very little.'

'No. It's just that ... your letter touched me very deeply.'

Maitri smiled, but didn't say anything. As usual, she was elegantly dressed. The powder-blue suit she had on was etched in gold, which struck me as slightly exotic. Her outfit gave her an oriental flavour that complemented her beautifully. Our conversation began slowly. I didn't really know what to say.

'I was just passing by,' I said, justifying my visit, 'and I felt like seeing you.'

'That's fine.'

We made our way into the living-room, and she offered me something to drink.

She left, and soon returned with some tea. After

hesitating a moment, I drank some. Her radiant eyes were upon me.

'And how is Susan?' she asked.

'Ah,' I sighed, somewhat sadly, 'I think my dream ... It's finished. I tried to see her several times, but she wasn't interested.'

'You didn't follow my instructions. I told you, "do nothing". That she would come. You didn't listen to me.'

'Your instructions seemed simple enough, but, in fact you misled me. It was easy for you to say, "Do nothing. Be happy. She will come."

'Don't do anything? The only problem with that is that I don't, or at least I didn't believe I could be happy without her. So, naturally, I ... but the more I think about it, the more I realise I was wrong about her. We're not meant for one another. We're not meant to be together. Otherwise, we would be.'

'Why do you say that? Why have you given up so easily? Who says she's not for you?'

'She very well may be, but I'm tired of waiting for her. I'm going to try and be happy with someone else.'

'So soon? Even though you've been waiting twelve years? Aren't you willing to wait another few weeks? What are a few weeks compared with a whole lifetime? Why do you have so little faith? When you've planted a seed and the seed is noble and right, do you constantly have to worry whether wheat will grow when summer comes? If you have any doubts, isn't it because you don't love this woman?'

'I love her, but ... Well, I'm not sure any more. I can't spend my whole life waiting. Besides, when I think about it, we weren't really meant to live together. We're so different!'

'Would you really want to spend the rest of your life with someone just like you?'

'No, but ... Damn it! I can't talk about it any more! Why couldn't things be simpler?'

'But they are', Maitri said, sitting beside me. 'It's your heart that's confused. Have you forgotten what I told you, that what you experience in love is a perfect mirror of your own heart?'

'So why go on wondering, as if it's all so mysterious, as if we're talking about the mysteries of life, when what we're really talking about is *you* and *your* problems?

'Look at yourself. Look at your life, and you'll find the cause of your heartache. And if you're wondering about it all, look again into your heart.'

'I've really tried to do that, but it's not easy.'

'I've told you, the easiest way to elevate your mind is through meditation. Your mantra is the boat that will help you cross the sea, get you to the Other Side, to the Golden Coast where there are no more worries.

'Don't think that I'm just talking nonsense, that these are just empty words. What all the wise men have said is true. Do you think I'd tell you such things if they weren't? Why? What would I gain?'

'I don't know.'

'Certainly, nothing valuable in the eyes of ordinary men. Over time, I've learned to live by a superior law, as have my brothers.'

I drank some more tea. I felt uncomfortable.

'The purpose of my life,' she went on, 'is to lead those who are ready to a state beyond all limitations. Don't be fooled. When your head tells you, "that's impossible", it's not. Listen to your heart. You can find true happiness.'

'But there are so many selling dreams, these days!' I protested.

I heard a rustling sound behind me, and turned around. Two very imposing men wearing long white robes and sandals were standing at the back of the room. They had a noble presence, as noble and majestic as Maitri's, and their faces were as radiant as hers. I hadn't the slightest idea how they got there. I didn't hear them come in.

'These are my brothers', Maitri said.

'P–Pleased to meet you', I stammered.

They said nothing, and nodded respectfully. It was hard to tell how old they were. Something about their bodies made them seem ageless. One of them, however, seemed younger than the other. He spoke in a weak, but melodious voice.

'You're late, Maitri.' There was no reproach in his voice, only kindness and compassion.

'I know', she replied. 'But I haven't finished what I had to do.'

'We know', they responded in unison. 'We're here to help you.'

'Leonard, this is Emile and this is Jost', Maitri introduced us.

'Nice to meet you, both of you.'

'You seem rather nervous today', Emile said. 'Well, that's OK. We've been watching you for years. Our mission is to make you one of us.'

I was becoming very frightened.

What did he mean? I felt as if I were in a dream. I remembered something I'd recently read in a book by Spalding, *Lives of the Masters*. He talked about two Masters called Jost and Emile. Was this just a coincidence?

Could these two, who had appeared so inexplicably without warning, be those Masters endowed with supernatural powers, materialising at will wherever they chose? Was this some kind of sci-fi fantasy?

'Come,' Maitri said, 'follow me. We must do what must be done.'

I got up and followed her to a small, all-white room. There was no furniture in it. But on the walls were a lot of photographs, all of them extraordinarily beautiful and of radiant people.

'Who are they?' I asked her.

'They are friends, brothers', she told me.

I was astonished when I recognised someone. It was the surrealist poet André Breton. He must have been about thirty when the picture was taken. And what was most amazing about it is the fact that Maitri was at his side!

But she looked exactly the same age in the photograph, about thirty, as now! If Breton were still alive, he would be over seventy. So, Maitri must be at least that age!

'Is that really you with Breton?' I asked.

'Yes. His poetic explorations would have brought him greater emancipation if he hadn't stopped along the way. True poetic genius is simply another form of mysticism. Breton was a man with great talent. There was a time when we believed we could work with him more. His world fame tempted him away. But he'll return, and we'll be able to use his talent for its originally intended purpose. Life is a slow progression.'

Her long-winded reply made me forget what I'd asked, but now it came back to me.

'How old were you at the time?'

'No older than I am now. Age is only an illusion. Once we accept that life is eternal, that we never die, but simply take on different external forms, and most of all when we obey the superior Law of Love, we can rise above the tyranny of time.

'When perfect love resonates within us, we can retain our body to accomplish certain tasks, to save time. It's that simple ... but you'll find out for yourself. Enough of this. Do you know why you're here?'

'No, I'm not sure I do. I thought I was ... uh ...'

'You took a great step when you understood that human love means suffering. Yet, you desperately continued your search for love. Now freedom is at stake. And I must ask you, 'Do you want to receive initiation into perfect love?'

I didn't know what to say. But something compelled me to say, 'Yes. Yes, I do.'

'Then say, "I want to be initiated!"'

'Maitri, I want to be initiated!'

'Very good! Now you'll never be the same again.'

Then Maitri's brothers, Emile and Jost, entered the room. I thought that this ceremony would be a private one, but Maitri apparently had decided otherwise. Emile and Jost came and stood beside me, Emile to my left, Jost to my right.

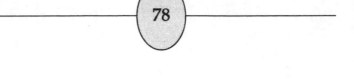

Maitri then asked: 'Emile, do you accept the responsibility of this new brother?'

'Yes, I do.'

'Jost, do you accept the responsibility of this new brother?'

'Yes, I do.'

Each of them took me by the hand, and stood silent and motionless beside me.

Then Maitri looked straight into my eyes. She stared at me. Raising her hand, she held out her right index finger and for an instant seemed transfixed. Then, with a quick wave of her hand she touched her finger to my heart.

I felt that my heart would explode, so violent was the upheaval within me. I felt as if I were going to pass out. Tears filled my eyes. I was charged with a tremendous surge of love, unlike anything I'd ever experienced before.

Seconds later, Maitri took her finger away. The fire in her eyes slowly faded, and her two brothers let go of my hands. But I continued to cry, still washed by great waves of love – an incomparable, objectless love. Was this the love that Maitri had spoken so much about?

'Come, follow me', she said. I followed her back to the living-room, accompanied by her two brothers.

'Now, we must go. We're already late.'

'Will I see you again?' I asked her.

'Not for a few years, but that's not important. But

you may see my brothers again. Now, they are your brothers, too. We are spread out throughout the world. In the days to come, you'll face many new challenges.'

'But what should I do? I'll be all alone!'

'No, from now on, you'll never be alone again. And a woman, one of our sisters, will help you. She's the door to perfect love.'

'Who is she? What's her name? How will I recognise her?'

'You'll know. She's close by. She'll help you.'

Then Maitri handed me the little book she'd always kept with her.

'This is for you, a memento', she said.

I thanked her.

Then Jost approached me. He was holding an exquisite black case with a quarter-moon jewel on its cover.

'This is a gift from us', he said, as he handed it to me. 'Always keep it with you. It will bring you luck wherever you go. Each of us has one. It has the secret power to answer whatever question you may have. But it works only once. So choose your question wisely. To find your answer, just open it.'

That was all he said. I sincerely thanked him, although I wasn't really sure how valuable this gift was. But it seemed practical enough, and certainly unique, if its alleged powers were genuine.

'Now we must go', Maitri said. 'It'll be a long time

before we meet again. But you no longer need me. I've given you what I was supposed to.'

'How can I ever thank you?'

'Go, and in everything you do, abide by the Law of Love. There is none higher.'

One after the other, Maitri's brothers approached, embraced me and kissed me on the cheeks. Then she did the same. I was deeply moved. It was the most touching farewell.

Maitri left, with her brothers behind her. I followed them. As I pulled the door shut, I clumsily dropped the case. I let out a cry and stooped to pick it up, hoping I hadn't damaged it. I was relieved to find it wasn't broken, wasn't even scratched.

But as I turned around, much to my surprise, Maitri and her brothers had disappeared. I looked up and down the street, but saw no one. Where did they go?

Recovering from my astonishment, I returned to my apartment, carrying the precious case I'd been given.

In the days that followed, I went through a tremendous change, just as Maitri had said I would. The surges of love I'd experienced when she'd touched my heart still flowed through me.

All the ugliness in my life appeared before me. I saw that my heart had been filled with hatred, in spite of my apparent good nature.

What Nirvana means now seems clear to me. It is

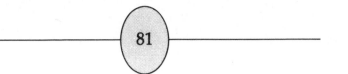

the end of all becoming, of all desire, of all hatred.

The many contradictions of my life suddenly disappeared. The memory of my former lovers would no longer torment me. I'd gone beyond my disappointment, what I'd failed to reconcile.

When I thought about my lovers, a great wave of tenderness now swept over me, as if I were loving them for the very first time. And I understood that if I'd left them, believing none of them was *the* love of my life, it wasn't their fault.

In retrospect, they all seemed worthy of much more. True. I could have stayed with them, and I could have been happy. My only problem was, I didn't love them enough.

So often, I'd been afraid of committing myself, dreading the ennui, the banality of marriage. I'd been afraid of its finality. But the truth was that I'd yet to discover the infinite, the absolutely right person, the total relationship.

And finding it suddenly in myself, and being at peace, I found it in an Other. In fact, I found it in all Others. And, as a result, I was starting from scratch, starting all over again.

I was infinitely grateful to Maitri for this. And I so much wanted to thank her that I decided to return to her place, even though she'd told me she wouldn't see me again for quite a long time. Still, I hoped she'd be at home, and above all, that she would see me again.

I went back to her place two days later. I went up to the door and rang the bell. A woman in her forties answered.

'Yes?' she asked. She seemed a little annoyed and surprised by my visit.

'Is Maitri at home?'

'Maitri? I think you've got the wrong house.'

I stepped back to check the address. No, it was the right one.

'I'm sure she lives here', I said. 'At least, she lived here two days ago. I guess she moved. I hope you don't mind me asking, but how long have you lived here?'

The woman looked insulted.

'Well! We've been living here for five years. And I've never heard of anyone by that name.'

'I'm sorry, I—I'm just trying to work this thing out. You see, I came here just two days ago and ... Could I come in for a minute?'

The woman hesitated, then let me in. I wasn't dreaming, was I? What? What had happened? The living-room, the ... it was different. It was crowded with furniture, in rather poor taste. A man entered the room. he was obviously her husband.

'What does *he* want?' the man asked his wife.

'He claims some woman was living here, and ...'

'Just on Monday. But I must've made a mistake. Sorry if I caused you any trouble.'

'No problem', the husband assured me. 'You must

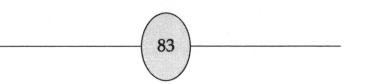

have just got the address mixed up. It can happen to anyone.'

I apologised profusely, and was just about to leave when into the room bounded the most charming little girl, perhaps twelve or so. She gave me a big smile, as though she knew me, or really liked me right away. I said, 'Hello', and complimented her. 'What a terrific smile you have! What a beautiful little girl you are!'

I was on my way out, but I felt something strange was going on, and I suddenly noticed the bracelet the little girl was wearing. A shiver ran up my spine. It was the same one Philippa had given me – I mean, that Susan handed me during the incredible dream state, the memory Maitri had brought about in me in this very house!

'Let me ask you a question?' I knelt in front of the little girl.

'OK', she said, and grinned, as if she knew what I was going to ask her.

'Oh, what a pretty bracelet! Where'd you get it?'

Her father didn't like my question at all. He undoubtedly thought it was a bit strange.

'Susan, return to your room immediately. Your punishment's not over yet!' her father said impatiently.

My thoughts ran a mile a minute! Another Susan wearing the same bracelet? I'm dreaming again? No. There's something funny going on here. This is just too coincidental! What the hell is going on?

But the way the girl's father looked at me, I decided that I had better go. Little Susan moved away. Then she flashed her smile again, turned and ran out of the room.

'Sorry for having bothered you', I apologised once more, and left. Once outside, I checked the address on the door again. It was definitely the right one. Maybe I was on the wrong street? I ran to the nearest sign. But it was the right one! I returned to my place, baffled.

I spent the rest of the day busily writing down what had happened, putting down every last detail. I kept thinking, 'How bizarre!' And 'Boy! Those people had moved in awfully fast!'

And I thought, 'What about that little girl being Susan and wearing the same bracelet as ...? God! That bracelet's worth a fortune, and for a kid to be wearing it!'

'I'm going nuts! Nothing happened. There's no

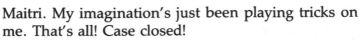

Maitri. My imagination's just been playing tricks on me. That's all! Case closed!

'But wait a minute! What about the black box? It's sitting right here on the table in front of me.'

I examined it carefully. If it really possessed psychic powers, as Maitri's brother had claimed, why not ask it if Maitri was just a figment of my imagination? Whether she was real or make-believe?

But I could only ask one question. Wouldn't it be stupid to ask such a silly one? For deep inside me I had no doubt I'd met her, even if I couldn't explain why her house was now inhabited by a family claiming to have lived there for five years.

It would surely be better to ask this magic box a more basic question. I spent a good part of the evening puzzling over what question to ask.

I considered different ones. I was playing a little game, one I'd never played before. When would the moment of my death come? No, that point in time didn't really interest me. Besides, what good would knowing that do? I couldn't change it anyway.

I still had to know one thing – was Susan going to be a part of my life? Maitri had promised she would, provided I didn't chase after her and that I was happy. Before I didn't think that was possible. Now ...well. Maybe it was. Maitri had unveiled my heart at my initiation, had propelled me to a plane of consummate happiness I'd never even believed possible before. Words can't describe it.

What's more, I'm sure that just three days ago, if I'd read this, I wouldn't have understood a thing. It's not easy to say what you mean. Descriptions don't tell us everything. You have to go through the experience, otherwise you have to accept it on blind faith.

Still looking at the black case, I kept telling myself, 'Ask about Susan! Is she going to marry me? Or, maybe I'd be happier with someone else? What's love?' There was no end to the questions I could ask!

I recalled my memories with Susan. Actually, we hadn't shared all that much! A few hours together, some phone calls, an innocent kiss or two that I'd practically had to steal from her. What else, but waiting and dreaming?

But now, in a different state of mind, I didn't feel the slightest resentment towards her. Well, except for the fact that she didn't say 'No' to me right away, she really wasn't to blame. I started thinking about her, the most tender thoughts. My obsession with her also disappeared. And the whole affair that'd had me in its grip just days ago now seemed part of a distant, almost forgotten past.

If I saw Susan again, in a way it would be as if we'd never met before, because I'd undergone a complete inner transformation.

These reflections and conjectures gradually began to fade away. My mind, that troublesome machine, was grinding to a halt. I remember what Maitri had said, the startling yet simple guiding principle? 'When you love someone, they love you.'

And now I understand that the only question we really need to ask about a person is whether or not WE love them. Nothing else matters.

I was holding the black case in my hands, and wondering – How can it answer my question if I no longer know what it is? Enough, I got up to go.

My heart was at peace. Susan crossed my mind, like a dear friend might, like a sister might, and I went to put the box away, as if I'd forgotten its amazing powers. The telephone rang. It didn't trigger the love-sick anguish I had known.

Suddenly, to my astonishment, it was as if I forgot everything. For the first time in my life, I felt truly alive.

THE END